Reflecting on Group Experiences at University and College

A Workbook for Final-Year Students

Adam Morgan

Sydney, Australia

Copyright © 2023, 2025 Adam Morgan

All rights reserved. Except to the extent permitted by law, no part of this publication may be reproduced, distributed, or transmitted in any form or by any means, including photocopying, recording, or other electronic or mechanical methods, without the prior written permission of the author. The author can be contacted via adam-morgan.com.au.

The information contained in this workbook is for educational purposes. No warranties of any kind are declared or implied. By engaging with this workbook, the user agrees that under no circumstances is the author responsible for any damages or losses, direct or indirect, that are incurred as a result of the use of the information contained within this workbook, including, but not limited to, errors, omissions, or inaccuracies.

ISBN 978-0-6456794-7-2

Published by Adam Morgan

Design and Layout:
Ilka Staudinger-Morgan

Contents

Introduction		1
Part A	**Considering Experiences**	**3**
	1. Group Goals	4
	2. Group Meetings	6
	3. Leadership	8
	4. Followership	10
	5. Helping	12
	6. Effort Reduction	14
	7. Conflict	16
	8. Cohesion	18
	9. Diversity	20
Part B	**Reconsidering Experiences**	**23**
	10. Most Memorable Group Experience	24
	11. Development of Teamwork Abilities	26
	12. Strongest Teamwork Abilities	28
	13. Areas Needing Further Improvement	30
	14. Learning Through Participation in Group Work	32
Conclusion		35
References		36

Introduction

This workbook will help you reflect on your group experiences at university/college. It works on the assumption that you have worked with others in groups during your studies (e.g., in assignment groups, project teams, discussion groups, study groups, and co-curricular/extracurricular activity groups). Each time you worked with others in groups, you had experiences—group experiences. Throughout these pages, you will reflect on some of these group experiences.

Completing this workbook is straightforward. First, you will consider your group experiences against various group-related topics and write accounts. Later, you will reconsider what you have written so that you can draw more meaning from your experiences.

After completing this workbook, you will have captured many important in-sights into group work and what you have experienced. You will have identified some of your strengths when working with others and some areas needing improvement. You will also have the necessary words to describe yourself and your group experiences when required in the future (e.g., in a job interview).

This workbook requires you to write entries. In terms of the amount you write and the quality of your entries, this depends on how you have come about engaging with this workbook. If you are completing this workbook as part of your personal development, with no institutional expectations or requirements, then the amount you write and the quality of your entries is your decision. You can write as little or as much as you like in the spaces provided, and the quality of your entries is also up to you. If completing this workbook is required at your institution, however, it is important that you clarify what is expected of you. There might be specific expectations regarding the amount you have to write and the quality of your entries.

The ability to write entries in this workbook will vary. Some will find it easy, whereas others might find it more challenging. If you are stuck or looking for suggestions, some 'you might like to consider' prompts are given. They are just suggestions to help if needed. You do not need to address every prompt given.

Part A

Considering Experiences

In the first part of this workbook, nine group-related topics are presented. These are:

- Group Goals
- Group Meetings
- Leadership
- Followership
- Helping
- Effort Reduction
- Conflict
- Cohesion
- Diversity

Your task is to write entries on these topics based on your group experiences. Remember, writing your entries can be challenging. It is normal to think, "I don't know where to begin." Try not to write immediately. Take some time to think about the prompts. Think of drafting your responses. Pretend you are going to be interviewed, and the interviewer has given you the questions in advance. When you see "write about…," you should pretend that the interviewer is asking, "Tell me about…." If you can say it, you should be better able to write it.

1. Group Goals

In most instances, groups have a goal to achieve, and members contribute to this goal. Members typically make specific contributions to the goal through the tasks they are allocated to perform. These tasks are usually connected or merged with other members' contributions to form an integrated whole. Each member's part contributes to the group's goal.

In the space on the next page, write about your experiences of group goals and contributing to them. You might like to consider:

- The types of goals your groups had (e.g., writing a report together, making a presentation together, making something together).
- How your groups decided who did what to achieve goals.
- The challenges you had with the allocation of tasks.
- The types of contributions you typically made in groups.
- How the other group members received your contributions.
- Your commitment to group goals.
- Other members' commitment to group goals.
- How group goals compare to individual goals.
- What was your most memorable group goal?
- What made it memorable?

My experiences of group goals and contributing to them:

2. Group Meetings

To achieve their goals, groups usually need to meet, either face-to-face or virtually. In meetings, members communicate with one another for various reasons. For example, they share ideas, discuss issues, make decisions, provide updates on progress, raise concerns, bring others into discussions, solve problems, or allocate new tasks. Even though a particular person might chair a meeting, all members are expected to participate in group meetings.

In the space on the next page, write about your experiences of group meetings and your participation in them. You might like to consider:

- How many group meetings did you participate in during your studies?
- For how long did your group meetings usually last?
- Where did your meetings take place?
- Overall, how productive were your meetings?
- What made your meetings productive/unproductive?
- What were the main challenges your groups faced during meetings?
- How did you overcome these challenges?
- What did you enjoy about group meetings?
- How do meetings help groups?
- What was your most memorable group meeting?
- What made it memorable?

My experiences of group meetings and participating in them:

3. Leadership

Groups in workplaces typically have formally appointed leaders. This person usually calls and runs meetings, allocates work, deals with issues, and liaises with various stakeholders. In student groups, such responsibilities are often left up to the members to perform. Sometimes, these leadership duties are given to a particular person (i.e., the elected leader). On other occasions, the responsibilities are shared or distributed within the group.

In the space on the next page, write about your experiences of leadership in groups. You might like to consider:

- The typical leadership structure in your groups (e.g., allocated to a member, shared/distributed).
- The main types of leadership duties played by group members.
- The role that leadership played in your groups.
- How leadership helped/hindered your groups.
- The challenges of leading in student groups.
- The skills needed to lead in student groups.
- How acts of leadership are received by others in groups.
- The extent to which you performed leadership duties in your groups?
- If you did lead, what was the result? How did you feel?
- If you did not lead, what prevented you? How did you feel?
- A memorable moment of leadership in one of your groups.
- What made it memorable?

My experiences of leadership in groups:

4. Followership

In the previous task, you wrote about leadership in your groups. In this task, you will consider the other side of leadership: followership. When acts of leadership are performed, others typically respond by doing what is requested. They attend the scheduled meetings, provide input when asked, and perform the tasks asked of them. Following should not be viewed as a passive, docile activity. It is active and purposeful. When members follow, they support those attempting to lead, which helps the group progress.

In the space provided on the next page, write about your experiences of followership in groups. You might like to consider:

- The extent to which members followed the lead of others in your groups.
- The benefits of members following the lead of others.
- The downsides/challenges of members following.
- The extent to which you followed the lead of others.
- If you followed, what was the result? How did you feel?
- If you did not ever follow, why didn't you? What was the result?
- A memorable moment of followership in one of your groups.
- What made it memorable?

My experiences of followership in groups:

5. Helping

When group members perform their allocated duties, they often face challenges. Sometimes, members work through their challenges and overcome them independently. On other occasions, they require help, and this help usually comes from a fellow group member. The person in need of assistance might request the help. That is, they see they have a problem and reach out for help. In other instances, a fellow group member considers the situation and offers to help. Either way, help is provided from one member to another. It helps the member in need and the group.

In the space on the next page, write about your experiences of helping in groups. You might like to consider:

- The extent to which members helped one another in your groups.
- The benefits of members' helping one another.
- The downsides/challenges of helping other group members.
- The extent to which others helped you in your groups.
- If you were helped, how did this come about? What was the result? How did you feel?
- The extent to which you helped others in your groups.
- If you did help, how did this come about? What was the result? How did you feel?
- If you did not help, why didn't you?
- A memorable moment of helping in one of your groups.
- What made it memorable?

My experiences of helping in groups:

6. Effort Reduction

It is quite common for group members to reduce their effort occasionally. Sometimes, this reduction is slight, such as when a member 'has their mind elsewhere' and says little in a meeting. In other instances, the effort reduction is significant, like when a member fails to attend meetings or delivers work late. The reason for this reduction can also vary. It might have arisen through no fault of the group member. For example, they were sick and had no choice but to reduce their effort. Alternatively, the reduction might have been more strategic. Here, the 'free rider' appears to have put their efforts elsewhere. Some groups react by insisting that the free-riding person increases their effort and performs their allocated duties (to varying levels of success). Others respond by 'taking up the slack' and doing more than their fair share of the work.

In the space on the next page, write about your experiences of effort reduction in groups. You might like to consider:

- The extent to which you experienced effort reduction.
- What sort of effort reduction did you experience?
- Why do you think effort reduction occurred?
- How did you/the group respond to the effort reduction?
- What was the result?
- How did the effort reduction affect your group?
- How did you feel when you experienced effort reduction?
- Did you ever reduce your effort in a group?
- If yes, in what way did you reduce your effort? Why did you reduce your effort?

My experiences of effort reduction in groups:

7. Conflict

Conflict is a common occurrence in groups. Conflict sometimes arises through disagreements about what the group needs to do (i.e., the task itself) or how it should be done (i.e., the process). Alternatively, conflict might be more relationship-oriented, with members clashing somehow. Conflict might be very brief, or it might last a long time. It might involve all group members or just a few. You might have been involved in the conflict (e.g., a central player). Alternatively, you might have observed other members involved in the conflict.

In the space on the next page, write about your experiences of conflict in groups. You might like to consider:

- The extent to which you experienced conflict.
- What sort of conflict did you experience?
- How long did the conflict last?
- Why do you think the conflict occurred?
- How did you/the group respond to the conflict?
- What was the result?
- How did the conflict affect your group?
- How did you feel when you experienced conflict?
- Were you directly involved in a conflictual situation in a group?
- If yes, why did it occur? What happened? How did it affect you and the group?

My experiences of conflict in groups:

8. Cohesion

Members of groups often bond together. In group dynamics, a bonded group is called a cohesive group (Forsyth, 2019). In cohesive groups, members like each other and enjoy working together. Sometimes, this bonding develops gradually as trust, success, and momentum develop. In other cases, members 'click' and form into a cohesive unit very early in the group's life and stay this way until disbanding.

In the space on the next page, write about your experiences of cohesion in groups. You might like to consider:

- The extent to which you experienced group cohesion.
- If you experienced cohesion, how did the cohesion arise?
- How did it benefit or hinder the group?
- How long did it last for?
- How did you feel when you participated in a cohesive group?
- If you did not experience cohesion, why did cohesion fail to arise in your groups?
- How did a lack of cohesion help or hinder your groups?

My experiences of cohesion in groups:

9. Diversity

Working with other students at your institution meant working in diverse groups. Sometimes, this diversity may not have been immediately apparent. For example, you looked similar and had the same first language. But diversity was still there at the deeper, less visible level. Your values and personalities would have been quite different, for example. On other occasions, the diversity in your groups was more evident. Your fellow group members might have been different in terms of their ethnicity, attitudes, and beliefs, to name a few.

In the space on the next page, write about your experiences of diversity in groups. You might like to consider:

- What sort of diversity was present in your groups?
- What were the challenges of working in diverse groups?
- What were the benefits of working in diverse groups?
- What was the result of having this diversity?
- How did you feel when you experienced diversity?
- A memorable moment involving diversity in one of your groups.
- What made it memorable?

My experiences of diversity in groups:

Part B

Reconsidering Experiences

In Part A of this workbook, you wrote entries based on your group experiences. In this second part, you will now reconsider these entries. This reconsidering is a very important part of the reflective process. It will help you see the bigger picture and draw many of your group experiences together. Before we begin Part B, it is essential that you re-read your entries. Once you have done this, there are five more short tasks to complete. These relate to your:

- Most Memorable Group Experience
- Development of Teamwork Abilities
- Strongest Teamwork Abilities
- Areas Needing Further Improvement
- Learning Through Participation in Group Work

Most of these tasks have some more 'you might like to consider' prompts to assist you. As in Part A, you do not need to address every prompt given.

10. Most Memorable Group Experience

You wrote entries related to various group-related topics in the previous part of this workbook (Part A). Each of these entries captured aspects of your group experiences. Some of these experiences are likely positive, whereas others may have been less positive. It is now time to consider what your most memorable group experience was.

In the space on the next page, describe your most memorable group experience during your studies. You might like to consider:

- The experience where you grew the most.
- The experience where you did something exceptional.
- The experience that you enjoyed the most.
- The experience that was the most challenging for you.
- A time when your group had excellent dynamics.

You might also like to consider explaining:

- Why it was your most memorable experience?
- How did the experience come about?
- How did the experience make you feel?
- What did you learn from the experience?

My most memorable group experience:

11. Development of Teamwork Abilities

Your educational institution has given you the opportunity to work with others in groups. By working in groups, you could learn from your peers, interact with others in your cohort, and develop a stronger sense of belonging, to name a few. You were also provided with the opportunity to develop your teamwork abilities. Your entries in the previous part of this workbook should have captured some of this development. Stating which ones have been the most developed is your next task.

In the space on the next page, write about which teamwork abilities have been most developed through your participation in group work. You might like to consider the extent to which you developed some of the following abilities*:

- Listening actively
- Communicating constructively
- Helping
- Leading
- Following the lead of others
- Treating others with respect
- Responding to conflict
- Motivating others
- Contributing to group meetings
- Working as a problem-solver
- Showing flexibility
- Demonstrating reliability
- Fostering constructive group climates

* Drawn from frameworks proposed by Brounstein (2002), Wheelan (2015), and the Association of American Colleges and Universities (AAC&U).

The development of my teamwork abilities:

12. Strongest Teamwork Abilities

Most employers today look for people who can work well with others in teams. If you look at job advertisements, they often state that strong teamwork abilities are an essential requirement. You might even see the following: A demonstrated ability to work well in teams. Your entries in the previous part of this workbook should have captured some of these abilities. Your previous entry on the development of your teamwork abilities might have also captured some of your strengths.

In the space on the next page, write about your strongest teamwork abilities. You might like to consider:

- The topics covered in Part A (e.g., leading, helping others, following the lead of others).
- The abilities mentioned most often in your entries.
- The abilities you have developed the most.
- How this development came about.

My strongest teamwork abilities:

13. Areas Needing Further Improvement

In the previous task, you stated your strongest teamwork abilities. You should also consider the other side: some areas where improvements are needed. Working with others in groups is challenging. Nobody is perfect at it. We all struggle in various places. Some of these areas might have arisen in your entries or crossed your mind when you were writing them. Writing about a few of these room-for-improvement areas is your next task.

In the space on the next page, write about some of your teamwork abilities that might need further improvement. You might like to consider how you:

- Managed your work and performed your duties.
- Interacted with others in your groups.
- Reacted to issues arising in your groups (e.g., conflict, the reduction of effort).
- Rate against the list of abilities presented on page 26. Which of these are your weakest?

You might also like to consider how you could improve any of the identified areas.

My teamwork abilities needing further improvement:

14. Learning Through Participation in Group Work

The author of this workbook once had a conversation with the manager of a careers unit at a university. During this conversation, the manager mentioned worrying feedback received from graduate recruiters. The recruiters were disappointed with the ability of students to talk about their group experiences. The students could say that they had participated in group work but could not say what they had learned through their participation in group work.

Having completed this workbook, you should be well-equipped to express what you have learned through your participation in group work. Currently, what you have learned is scattered throughout this workbook. Bringing it into one place is your final task.

In the space on the next page, write about what you have learned through your participation in group work.

What I have learned through my participation in group work:

Conclusion

This workbook has allowed you to reflect on some of your group experiences at university/college. Some of your experiences now exist on the pages of this workbook. You have recalled various experiences and have engaged with them in a structured way. You should now be better able to use these captured experiences and the meanings you have drawn from them.

You should now be better able to describe who you are as a team player, which will assist you when populating CVs, completing professional profiles, and writing job applications. You should also be better able to handle team-related questions in job interviews. You now have the words needed to talk in an informed way when asked about your group experiences and what you have learned through your participation in group work. Just remember to re-visit the pages of this workbook in preparation for such interviews.

References

Association of American Colleges and Universities (AAC&U). *VALUE Rubrics - Teamwork*. Retrieved from https://www.aacu.org/initiatives/value-initiative/value rubrics/value-rubrics-teamwork

Brounstein, M. (2002). *Managing teams for dummies.* New York: Wiley.

Forsyth, D. (2019). *Group dynamics* (7th Ed.). Boston: Cengage.

Wheelan, S. A. (2015). *Creating effective teams: A guide for members and leaders* (5th Ed.). Thousand Oaks, CA: Sage.

www.ingramcontent.com/pod-product-compliance
Lightning Source LLC
Chambersburg PA
CBHW051158290426
44109CB00022B/2509